That was 1939

MARK JONES

Copyright © 2019 Mark Jones
All rights reserved.

CONTENTS

January – 7

February - 13

March – 17

April – 21

May – 27

June - 29

July - 31

August - 33

September – 35

October - 39

November - 45

December - 49

YOU NEED

FOX'S

Glacier REGT

MINTS

FOR THEIR
SUGAR VALUE

PER **6**d. QTR

THE FINEST PEPPERMINT IN
THE WORLD

REMEMBER 1914—1918

Don't forget to take a tin of
HARRISON'S POMADE
in your kit.
Kills all body vermin.

In tins, 6d. & 1/-, from all Chemists

1. JANUARY

Few years would prove to be as tumultuous as 1939. New years-day was grim in Germany, as in Berlin, the government ordered that all women under 25-years-old must do one years service for the Reich, the move proved very unpopular.

A few days later, the world famous pilot Amelia Earhart was officially declared dead after her disappearance – despite an extensive search, her body was never found. Meanwhile, in America, gangster Al Capone was moved from the prison island of Alcatraz to San Pedro on January 7th. He would be released soon after, and spend the rest of his life in seclusion.

A day later, on January 8th, church leaders in Germany were punished for condemning anti-Semitic events in the country. The following day, Hitler re-opened the Reichstag which had burned down in 1933, a crime which historian conclude he had a hand-in.

The diplomacy scene was busy as British Prime Minister visited Mussolini in Rome for talks on January 11th, the two men appeared to hit-it-off.

In Berlin, a shortage of coffee and jam saw housewives buying up all available supplies with the greatest possible speed, as most shops refused to sell more than a quarter of a pound of coffee at a time.

On the other side of the world in Australia, *Black Friday* killed 71 people across Victoria in one of the worst ever bushfires on January 13th – the incident left the country in deep shock.

In Moscow, Charles Lindbergh, the famed American pilot, was described as 'Hitler's Lackey', mainly due to his anti-communist rhetoric and praise of the Nazi authorities.

THAT WAS 1939

Life for Jews in Berlin took a drastic turn for the worse on January 17th when they were banned from visiting dentists, driving, keeping pets, or visiting cinemas and theatres.

A few days later, Egyptians celebrated as King Farouk was declared the 'spiritual leader of Islam.'

On January 24th, a deadly earthquake in Chile killed 30,000 – the rescue and clean up mission took months to complete. The next morning, the UK political scene was abuzz as Sir Stafford Cripps was expelled from the Labour Party.

MAYFAIR MARGARINE

On January 27th, Adolf Hitler ordered a five-year naval expansion programme intended to provide for a huge fleet capable of crushing the Royal Navy – it was an ambition he would never achieve.

Then, on January 30th, the RAF announced they were taking delivery of 400 new aircraft every month – a rise of 400 percent over one year.

In London, a committee on nurses concluded that most were overworked and underpaid a testament to the fact not much has changed since 1939.

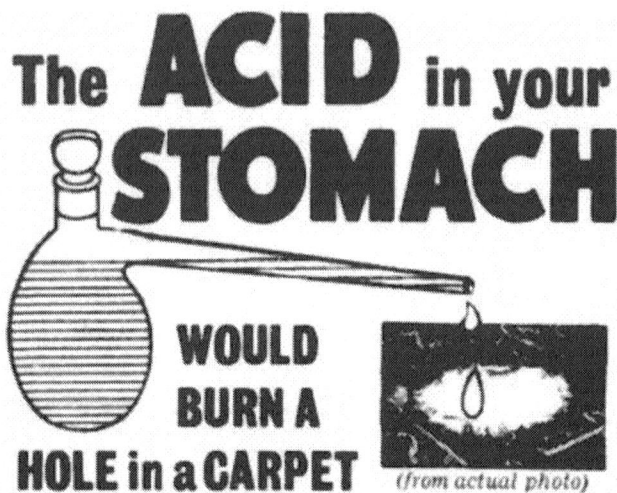

The ACID in your STOMACH WOULD BURN A HOLE in a CARPET *(from actual photo)*

After the kind of acid which causes indigestion had been poured on to a carpet, a hole appeared — *the acid had actually burned a hole as big as a saucer!* No wonder you suffer terrible burning pains when this dangerous acid attacks your tender stomach lining. To get relief, you must quickly rob excess acid of its deadly burning power.

2. FEBRUARY

On February 6th, the British Prime Minister Neville Chamberlain stated in the *House of Commons* that any German attack on France would be automatically considered an attack on Britain.

The signs of war where everywhere, on February 9th, free air-raid shelters began to be distributed to homes in areas most likely to be bombed in Britain. Families earning less than $250-a-year, received the shelters for free.

On February 10th, Pope Pius XI died of a heart attack in Rome – the Catholic world went into mourning.

'British soldiers of the future will have no buttons to clean, less puttees to wrap and a lighter pack to carry, and will dress in battle kit in half the time the 1914-18 soldier took', according to the *Daily Mirror*. In an article published on February 23rd, the paper said: 'Embodied in the left leg of the trousers is a large map pocket, similar those in flying clothes.'

On February 27th, *Borley Rectory* – the place dubbed 'the most haunted house in Britain – was destroyed by fire. The large Gothic-style rectory had been alleged to be haunted ever since it was built in 1862.

Meanwhile, the United Kingdom and France recognized Franco's government, prompting some MPs in the *House of Commons* to shout: 'Shame!'

3.MARCH

March started with the US government in Washington also recognizing the administration of Franco. On the West Coast, the drama film *The Little Princess* starring Shirley Temple premiered at Grauman's Chinese Theatre in Hollywood.

A day later, Marshall Petain, the French war hero, was named as ambassador to Spain.

On March 3rd, cinemagoers in the United States were treated to their first taste of the movie-star John Wayne in a leading role, when his feature *Stage Coach* was released. The following day in Germany, more restrictive measures were placed on Jews, when they were forcibly drafted to work for the Third Reich.

On March 10th, 20 terrorists belonging to the IRA were jailed in the UK for conspiracy to cause explosions. That same day, Czechoslovakian President Emil Hácha deposed Jozef Tiso as premier of the autonomous province of Slovakia and declared martial law.

There were major celebrations in Rome on March 12th, when the coronation of Pope Pius XII took place, many heard the event live around the world via *Vatican Radio*.

Instability increased in Europe three days later, when Hitler ordered his troops to march into Bohemia, then he declared Bohemia – Moravia a German protectorate. The event prompted a protest from London, and the recall of the British ambassador from Berlin. On March 19th, Pierre Montet announced the discovery of the *Tomb of Psusennes* I a few miles from Port Said in Egypt.

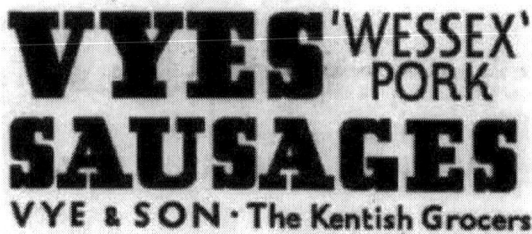

In sport, the horse *Workman* won the *Grand National* at Aintree, whist on March 26th, Britain's first commercial oil find was announced at Eakring in Nottinghamshire.

On March 31st, the Chamberlain government in London pledged Anglo-French support if Polish independence was threatened by Germany – it proved a promise which would change the course of world history.

4. APRIL

On April 1st, the nationalists in Spain officially declared an end to the Spanish Civil war, meanwhile, the German battleship *Tirpitz* was launched in Wilhelmshaven.

That same day, Cambridge won the 91st Boat Race. The race would not be officially held again until 1946.

On April 4th, *Glenn Miller and His Orchestra* recorded *Moonlight Serenade*, a piece of music which would become forever associated with the era.

On April 6th, Britain's largest aircraft carrier, *HMS Illustrious*, was launched at Barrow-in-Furness in Scotland. Meanwhile, Britain and France agreed on a mutual assistance pact with Poland, pledging to come to Poland's aid in the event of a German attack.

April 8th saw King Zog fleeing Albania to nearby Greece as Italian forces entered the capital Tirana, it took just a few days for the Italian army to complete the occupation of Albania.

On April 10th, Dutch troops were sent to the German border, whilst in Scotland, the city of Glasgow banned darts in pubs, be cause they were 'too dangerous'.

Across the continent, Moscow proposed an alliance with Britain and France to contain German aggression in Eastern Europe, it was an offer which was not accepted.

Meanwhile, a law was published in Italy proclaiming King Victor Emmanuel III's acceptance of the Crown of Albania.

On April 20th, Adolf Hitler's 50th birthday was celebrated as a national holiday throughout Germany – a huge parade took place through the streets of Berlin. Appropriately that day, Billie Holiday recorded a song called *Strange Fruit*.

On April 25th, the Chancellor of the Exchequer in London raised taxes to help finance the £630 million defense budget. That very same day, the Air Ministry announced that 761 recruits joined the RAF during the previous week compared with 250 in the corresponding period of 1938. This brought the total entry of pilots, observers, airmen, and boys since April 1st, 1939, to 1,781. The 761 entries were made of pilots and observers and 683 airmen.

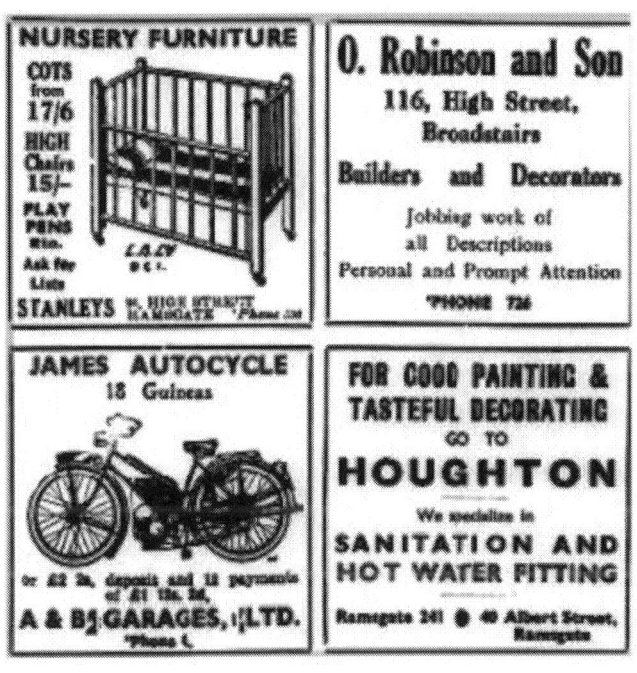

You will feel better and stronger and have more energy for your daily work *if you make* **Turog** Bread of Health your daily bread

Your baker bakes it Spillers

The fantasy classic the Wizard of Oz opened at Cinemas

Barely a day passed without Hitler being in the news.

Arthur Askey in 1939.

The King

5. MAY

On May 2nd, figures showed of the 180,000 Jews living in former Austria, 99,672 had emigrated, of which 20,677 went to North America and 6,194 to Palestine, according to the *Volkischer Beobachter*. On May 3rd, the British battleship *Prince of Wales* was launched in Birkenhead near Liverpool. Meanwhile, in the Nazi Germany, a speed limit for motor vehicles was introduced on May 7th.

On May 17th, the royal tour of Canada began when King George VI and Queen Elizabeth arrived in Quebec City – it was the first time a British monarch had visited Canada.

Across the border in the USA, NBC broadcast the first televised sporting event in North America, a baseball game between Princeton and

Columbia. The day after, the German Foreign Office announced the early conclusion of non-aggression agreements with Latvia, Estonia and Denmark.

On May 20th, *Pan-American Airways* began regular air mail service between the United States and Europe. Germany and Italy signed a ten-year military and political alliance known as the *Pact of Steel* on May 22nd. That same day, Chancellor Adolf Hitler told leading officers of the Wehrmacht about his plans for war at a meeting in the New Reich Chancellery in Berlin.

6. JUNE

The unfolding drama of the *St. Louis*, a cruise ship carrying a cargo of 907 Jewish refugees continued to unfold in early June. It was denied permission to land in Florida after already having been turned away from Cuba – for those on board, the situation was desperate.

Eventually, the vessel was forced to return to Europe and subsequently, many of its passengers later died in Nazi death camps.

RADIO SALE

Secondhand Receivers

Mostly part exchange models, in perfect working order, from—

£1 EACH

TOM JOYCE Radio Engineers

147, Boundary Road, Ramsgate Thane 1172

As this was happening, MGM's first successful animated character, *Barney Bear*, made his screen debut in *The Bear That Couldn't Sleep*. And in the USA, the *National Baseball Hall of Fame and Museum* was officially dedicated in Cooperstown, New York.

Meanwhile, war clouds were springing up everywhere. The Japanese began a blockade the British concession in Tianjin, China, beginning a crisis which almost caused an Anglo-Japanese war.

Back in Europe, the last public guillotining took place in France, when murderer Eugen Weidmann was executed, there were no mourners.

Further south, talks were completed in Ankara between French Ambassador René Massigli and Turkish Foreign Minister Şükrü Saracoğlu, resolving the Hatay dispute in Turkey's favour. The upshot was Turkey annexing Hatay.

On that same day, the government of Siam changed its name to Thailand, which means 'Free Land'.

7. JULY

Theodore Roosevelt's head is dedicated at Mount Rushmore.

The last remaining Jewish enterprises in Germany are closed by the Nazis. Soon after, thousands of Nazis held rallies in Danzig. District Leader Albert Forster declared he was confident that Hitler would "liberate" the city and demanded that Poland give up privileges of storing arms in a munitions depot on the Westerplatte.

On July 16th, British Fascist leader Sir Oswald Mosley gave a speech in the Earls Court Exhibition Centre attended by over 20,000 people. He presented a plan that he said would "bring peace in our time and our children's time" that called for a hands-off policy in Eastern Europe, disarmament in Western Europe, return of colonies to Germany and for the British Empire to concentrate on its own affairs.

The following week, the *Pan American Airways* Boeing 314 flying boat Yankee Clipper inaugurates the world's first heavier-than-air North Atlantic air passenger service between the United States and Britain.

Meanwhile, Mahatma Gandhi the spiritual leader from India writes a personal letter to Adolf Hitler addressing him "My friend", requesting to prevent any possible war.

The first recorded snowfall in Auckland, New Zealand since records began in 1853.

MARK JONES

8. AUGUST

The dark clouds of war began to loom over Europe, as the month began with 1,300 warplanes filling the skies over Britain on the first of several days of air defence tests.

King George VI conducted a fleet review of 133 ships at Weymouth Bay, on what a journalist described as a 'display of British naval might.' Around the same time, half of England went dark for four hours in a test to determine how effectively the country could shroud itself from enemy planes.

That very same day, the historical adventure film *Stanley and Livingstone* starring Spencer Tracy and Cedric Hardwicke premiered at Grauman's Chinese Theatre in Hollywood. A week later, the musical fantasy film *The Wizard of Oz* had its official premiere.

Meanwhile, Indian troops arrived in Egypt to strengthen British forces there, as German Navy boss Karl Dönitz received a coded instruction for his forces to put out to sea.

In the world of music, the song *You Are My Sunshine* was recorded for the first time, by the Pine Ridge Boys.

The very next day – August 23rd - the *Molotov–Ribbentrop Pact* was signed. Nazi Germany and the Soviet Union agreed not to attack each other and to remain neutral if attacked by a third power.

On August 30th, the Polish government ordered a

partial mobilization as in Britain the Royal Navy was mobilized and Army and Royal Air Force reserves were called up.

The signing of the Molotov- Ribbentrop Pact in Moscow.

9. SEPTEMBER

The world changed on September 1st, as the brutal German invasion of Poland began at 4:44 in the morning when the SMS Schleswig-Holstein opened fire on a garrison in Westerplatte, the first shots of World War II. The Luftwaffe began bombing raids on airfields, ships and troops.

Just two days later, at 11:15 a.m. Neville Chamberlain announced on BBC Radio that Britain and Germany were at war.

> You can imagine what a bitter blow it is to me that all my long struggle to win peace has failed", Chamberlain said, sounding dispirited. "Yet I cannot believe that there is anything more or anything different that I could have done and that would have been more successful ... We and France are today, in fulfillment of our obligations, going to the aid of Poland, who is so bravely resisting this wicked and unprovoked attack upon her people. We have a clear conscience. We have done all that any country could do to establish peace, but a situation in which no word given by Germany's ruler could be trusted and no people or country could feel themselves safe had become intolerable. And now that we have resolved to finish it, I know that you will all play your part with calmness and courage.

The following day, Winston Churchill accepted Chamberlain's offer to join his war cabinet as First Lord of the Admiralty. Churchill now held the same position he had at the outbreak of *World War I*.

On that very same day, the *Athenia* became the first UK ship to be sunk by Germany during *World War II*. 117 civilian passengers and crew were killed with the sinking condemned as a war crime. The dead included 28 US citizens, leading Germany to fear that the US might react by joining the war on the side of the UK and France.

In the United States, President Roosevelt declared a limited national emergency.

Increases were ordered in the enlisted strength of the army, navy and National Guard. Also, a $500,000 fund was allocated to assist in the return of American citizens stranded in war zones.

Meanwhile, in Berlin, rationing was stiffening. The diet of the German people for six years prior to the war had been gradually shifted towards a wartime level, so that the onset of direct rationing merely increased restrictions which had already been in force.

As all this was going on, the Glenn Miller and Ray Eberle version of *Over the Rainbow* topped the American pop charts as compiled by *Your Hit Parade*. At the same time, Patricia Donnelly of Michigan was crowned *Miss America* 1939.

On September 12th, the Duke and Duchess of Windsor returned to England from self-imposed exile in France. Just 24-hours later, the German submarine U-39 attacked the British aircraft carrier *HMS Ark Royal* off Rockall Bank, but the torpedoes fell short of their target. Three British destroyers in the vicinity hunted down U-39 and disabled it with depth charges, rescuing all the crew. It was the first U-boat to be sunk in *World War II.*

In the United States, famed aviator Charles Lindbergh made a nationwide radio broadcast in favour of American remaining in isolation:

> It is madness to send our soldiers to be killed as we did in the last war if we turn the course of peace over to the greed, the fear and the intrigue of European nations. We must either keep out of European wars entirely or stay in European affairs permanently", Lindbergh said. "We must not permit our sentiment, our pity, or our personal feelings of sympathy, to obscure the issue, to affect our children's lives ... America has little to gain by taking part in another European war.

YOU CAN'T GET 1¾ lbs. OF STEAK FOR 6d.

but you can get just as much energy from a ¼ lb. tin of FRY'S COCOA

10. OCTOBER

ON October 5th, Hitler flew to Warsaw and reviewed a victory parade in the fallen Polish capital. The following day, the *British Expeditionary Force* completed its crossing to France.

Black-Out To-night 6.13 p.m. until 7.39 a.m.

On October 16th, Nine planes of the Luftwaffe conducted an air raid on the Firth of Forth, damaging three British ships and killing sixteen Royal Navy crew.
 Meanwhile, the Soviet Union began its occupation of Estonia. A few days later, Some 2,000 Jews were deported from Nazi-controlled Vienna to Lublin in the General Government.' Newspapers reported that:

> A new independent State of Poland is to be formed as from November 1, according to the Berlin correspondent of the *Politiken*. The new State, will be about the size of Bulgaria. Its capital will be Warsaw. Three million Polish Jews collected from all over Poland are to be settled in a special Jewish State in the east. The capital of this State will he Lublin.

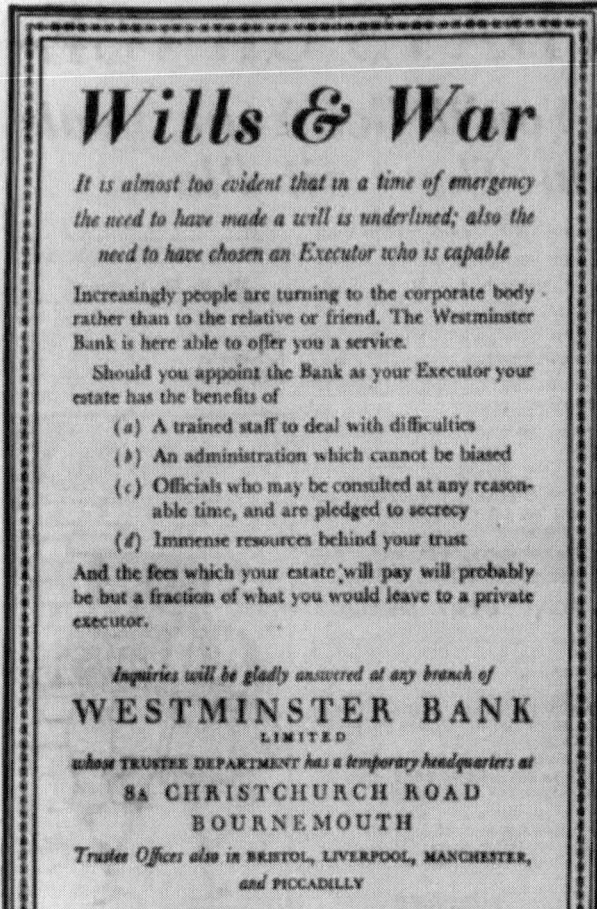

A Gallup poll result was published in the United States, asking, "Which side do you want to see win the war?" 84 percent of Americans surveyed said the Allies, 14 percent expressed no opinion, and only 2 percent said Germany.

MACLEANS
PEROXIDE
TOOTH PASTE

Obtainable everywhere 6ᵈ, 10½ᵈ and 1/6

Joachim von Ribbentrop made a speech in Danzig blaming Britain for the war and indicating that fighting would begin on a large scale now that Chamberlain had "refused the hand of the Führer stretched out in a peace gesture."

Away from the war, Gordon Selfridge, who started work as a grocer's became the world's most famous storekeeper, retired at the age of 74. And across the ocean, American pro football was televised for the first time when NBC broadcast a game between the Philadelphia Eagles and the Brooklyn Dodgers. The telecast was available to the approximately 500 television sets in the New York area and was also shown on monitors at the New York World's Fair. The hometown Dodgers won, 23-14. On October 28th, Heinrich Himmler issued a secret directive to the SS and police encouraging them to procreate with women of "good blood", even outside of marriage, "to regenerate life for Germany".

Meanwhile, a correspondent to a local newspaper observed:

> As the sirens screamed. heard some children shout: "Hooray! Now we can play in the air-raid shelter without being scolded".

11. NOVEMBER

A big joke of the day went like this...

> Have you heard Mrs. Goring's latest advice to German women? "
> " No, what is it? "
> "She told them not to wrap up their weekend joint in their bus ticket because it might fall through the punch hole."

At the start of the month, the U.S. Congress amended the *Neutrality Act*, repealing the embargo on arms to belligerents but placing sales on a cash and carry basis to avoid a repeat of the situation after *World War I* when Britain and France ran into difficulty with making their war debt payments to the United States.

Meanwhile, the British propaganda *film The Lion Has Wings*, was rushed through production after the outbreak of war, was released to cinemas in the United Kingdom.

On November 7th, Queen Wilhelmina of the Netherlands and King Leopold III of the Belgians offered to mediate in the war, but nothing came of the offer.

The following day there was high drama in Germany when 13 minutes after Hitler concluded a speech at the *Bürgerbräukeller*, a time bomb exploded near the speaking platform that killed 8 people. Carpenter Johann Georg Elser was arrested with incriminating documents at the Swiss border and brought back to Munich for interrogation.

His attempt to assassinate Hitler would have succeeded if the Führer's annual speech had not begun 30 minutes earlier than it did in previous years.

Al Capone

In the USA, Al Capone was released from federal custody on November 16th, after serving seven-and-a-half years of his eleven-year sentence for tax evasion. Capone was suffering heavily from paresis and upon release he immediately went to a Baltimore hospital for treatment.

That same day, the Dutch liner *Simon Bolivar* set off two mines and sank 20 miles off Harwich, England. 86 lives were lost out of the approximately 400 on board. On November 13th, British soil was bombed by the Germans for the first time, in the Shetland Islands. No casualties were inflicted. On November 21st, the British government declared a blockade of German exports in reprisal for numerous incidents at sea such as the sinking of the *Athenia* and the *Simon Bolivar*. Prime Minister Neville Chamberlain explained in the House of Commons:

> The many violations of international law and the ruthless brutality of German methods have decided us to follow a similar course now, and an Order-in-Council will shortly be issued giving effect to this decision.

On November 24th, *Imperial Airways* and *British Airways Ltd* merged to form *British Overseas Airways Corporation*. At the same time, the *International Olympic Committee* President Henri de Baillet-Latour announced the cancellation of the 1940 Winter Olympics, which would have been held in Garmisch-Partenkirchen, Germany.

On November 29th, a decree of the Presidium of the Supreme Soviet granted all permanent residents of Soviet-occupied Poland full citizenship of the USSR. With this came the obligation to serve in the Red Army. The month ended with the beginning of the Winter War, when the Soviet Union invaded Finland. 600,000 soldiers of the Red Army began to cross the Finnish border and Soviet aircraft bombed Helsinki.

BLACK·OUT TO·NIGHT

5.46 p.m.—7.43 a.m.

Light up an

Army Club

and nobody will run you
down in the dark

6½ᴅ. FOR **10** ★ 1'0½ᴅ. FOR **20**

12. DECEMBER

On December 3rd, 24 Vickers Wellington bombers raided German warships at Heligoland. A German anti-aircraft battery was hit, probably the first British bomb of the war to land on German soil. The next day, the German submarine U-36 was sunk by the British submarine Salmon.

On December 8th, the Roosevelt administration sent Britain a note protesting the British policy of seizing German goods on neutral ships.

Roosevelt

On a lighter note, the 1939 Nobel Prizes were awarded in Stockholm on December 10th. The recipients were Ernest Lawrence of the United States for Physics, Adolf Butenandt (Germany) and Leopold Ružička (Switzerland) for Chemistry, Gerhard Domagk (Germany) for Physiology or Medicine and Finn Frans Eemil Sillanpää for Literature. Unsurprisingly, the Peace Prize was not awarded.

The was high action on the seas during the *Battle of the River Plate*: In South American waters, the German cruiser *Admiral Graf Spee* was critically damaged in a battle with the British warships Exeter, Ajax and Achilles.

On December 14th, the Norwegian pro-Nazi politician Vidkun Quisling held meetings with Hitler and high-ranking members of the German military in Berlin as the Nazis probed ways to go about occupying Norway.

The following day, the epic romance *Gone with the Wind* starring Vivien Leigh, Clark Gable, Leslie Howard and Olivia de Havilland premiered at Loew's Grand Theatre in Atlanta.

On the 17th, the German cruiser *Admiral Graf Spee* was scuttled in neutral waters near Montevideo as the time limit to leave port was running out. Captain Hans Langsdorff believed that British reinforcements were nearby and that he had used up too much fuel and ammunition to fight his way back to Germany.

The next day, Adolf Hitler sent Joseph Stalin a telegram on his sixtieth birthday wishing him "good health and a happy future for the peoples of the friendly Soviet Union."

On December 20th, a fundraising rally for the Finnish Relief Fund called "Let's Help Finland" was held at *Madison Square Garden* in New York.

Herbert Hoover made a speech at the event which was also broadcast across the USA.

On December 22nd, two express trains collided in Magdeburg, Germany, killing at least 132 people.

On Christmas Eve, Pope Pius XII gave a Christmas address to 25 cardinals in which he offered a five-point program as a basis for negotiating a "just and honorable peace."

On New Year's Eve, celebrations in Britain, France and Germany were very subdued due to blackout and noise restrictions. Most gatherings were held in private homes with the windows shuttered.

An event that never happened

THAT WAS 1939

Printed in Great Britain
by Amazon